Easy Russian Alphabet

A Visual Workbook

Fiona McPherson, PhD

Published 2018 by Wayz Press, Wellington, New Zealand.

Copyright © 2018 by Fiona McPherson.

ISBN 978-1-927166-53-6

To report errors, please email errata@wayz.co.nz
For additional resources and up-to-date information about any errors, go to the Mempowered website at www.mempowered.com

Also by Dr McPherson

Indo-European Cognate Dictionary

Mnemonics for Study (2nd ed.)

My Memory Journal

How to Approach Learning: What teachers and students should know about
 succeeding in school

Successful Learning Simplified: A Visual Guide

How to Learn: The 10 principles of effective practice and revision

Effective Notetaking (3rd ed.)

Planning to Remember: How to remember what you're doing and what you plan
 to do

Perfect Memory Training

The Memory Key

Contents

Learning the letters

A few words on how we learn

How do we learn? Learning happens through two fundamental processes: connection, and repetition.

We always need repetition, but the amount of repetition needed varies a great deal. If we can make connections to information already well known to us, then that new information will be more easily remembered — meaning that it needs less repetition. For example, if your cousin has a new baby and names it Geraldine — a family name, the name of your aunt and great-aunt and great-grandmother — you will remember this much more easily than you would a less relevant name, chosen simply because the parents liked the sound of it.

When we learn meaningful topics, such as how genetic transmission occurs, or how black holes are formed, connections are made and strengthened in a way that reflects your growing understanding of the subject. When we learn something that is less rooted in meaning, such as vocabulary in a new language, reducing the amount of repetition required often depends on creating new, arbitrary connections.

The point of mnemonics (acronyms, images, silly stories) is to make arbitrary connections more memorable.

This book uses several strategies of proven effectiveness, in order to reduce the amount of repetition you need to learn the letters of the Russian alphabet. These strategies include grouping, mnemonic images, and opportunities for varied retrieval practice.

Grouping for memory

The standard way to learn an alphabet is as a list of letters in 'alphabetical order'. But a more effective way is to break it down into useful groups. I have broken down the Russian alphabet into groups based on how difficult the letters are to learn, for native users of the Roman alphabet (which is the one used by English speakers). Doing it this way not only enables you to more quickly master the bulk of the letters, it also explicitly tells you which letters need to be practiced more.

We're going to start with the easiest group — those which are just the same in both alphabets.

You may wonder why it's necessary to spend any time at all on these letters, which obviously you already know. There are two reasons. The first, and most important, is that there are some letters that are 'false friends' — that is, they look just like English letters, but they correspond to different sounds. It is not enough, therefore, to simply recognize the letters as the ones you're used to; you need to know that these are indeed the same letters you're familiar with. (Note that from now on I will use the word 'English' as a more user-friendly term for the Roman alphabet, given that this book is written in the English language.)

The second reason is that recognizing some letters is only good for the situation where you're reading the language. To write in it, you need to go further than recognition; you need to be able to produce the right letters. This means you need to know which letters represent which sounds.

The mnemonic cards

The foundation of your learning is the visual images I've constructed for each letter. Notice that each "card" shows, first, the upper and lower case forms of the Russian letter, written in a color picked out from the picture. Below these is the English letter that is translated as its equivalent. Below that is a word, in English,

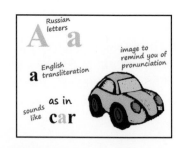

showing how that letter is pronounced. The part of the word that is the appropriate sound is written using the Russian letter. A picture showing the meaning of the word is then shown — not because the word is anything other than simple! but because images are generally much more memorable than words.

The key to learning the alphabet is to build a strong link between the image and the Russian letter. I'll talk more about this as we go. For now, let's have a look at the first group. This will give you the opportunity to see the strategy at work.

Group 1: Easy letters

A a

a

as in

car

К к

с

as in

кat

М м

m

as in

moon

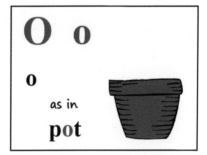

О о

o

as in

pot

Т т

t

as in

тop

These 5 letters are almost the same in the Russian alphabet as they are in ours, so they are the easiest to learn. The one exception is the K, but it is identical in shape to an English letter, and its transliteration (the letter it's translated into) matches an English letter that sometimes bears the same sound. The English c is (confusingly) sometimes 'soft' (s) and sometimes 'hard' (k). In Russian, then, the K is a hard c.

While the visual images are less important as memory aids for these easy letters, they do serve as reminders of pronunciation, particularly in the case of the K and the two vowels. The car for A reminds us that it is pronounced with a 'long' a sound, as in car and father. The pot for O reminds us that it's pronounced with a 'short' o sound, as in pot.

While the images for T and M may seem unnecessary, they will help you remember that these letters are exactly what they seem. Later we will learn several letters that are, on the contrary, not at all the familiar letters they appear to be.

The take-away from these first five cards, then, is that

- these are the 5 letters that are the same in both alphabets
- K = (hard) c, as in cat
- A is long, as in car
- O is short, as in pot.

> To remember which letters are the same in both languages, use the mnemonic: **ATOM K** (This is particularly appropriate, because ATOM is the same word in Russian.)

Group 2: Straightforward consonants

A very small set! This is really an appendix to group 1. These two letters are also relatively easy, with the first one in particular being almost one of the easy set: the letter for b is easily recognized as such, although not identical with ours. It is also pronounced in a similar way.

The letter for z is a little more problematic, since it most closely resembles a 3. You might use the mnemonic "3 zebras" or "three zees" to help you remember this.

How to practice

Mnemonic images and stories do help enormously, but if you look at them once and never again, they're going to fade from your mind quickly enough. You do need to rehearse them.

Which doesn't mean looking at them repeatedly! You need to actually retrieve them from your memory. This is a basic principle of learning: **only practice that involves retrieving items from your long-term memory helps you remember!**

The review sections, then, provide exercises for you to do this.

Calling them "reviews" is a little misleading, because they are not just a means to test your learning, but also a means of practicing *for* learning. How much practice you'll need will vary with the group — this first group should require very little. However, it's important to note that it's not simply a matter of getting the answers correct. Because letters need to be over-learned to the point of automaticity (so that you don't need to wonder, even fleetingly, what a letter is), you want to return to these reviews again and again, until you can answer them correctly instantly, without thought.

Variation is definitely a part of effective practice, which is why I provide another type of practice. After each review, you will find vocabulary sections, listing words that are mostly very similar to their English counterparts. (Some words may be harder to guess, but you can check out their meaning in the Glossary at the back of the book.) Practice reading these words at intervals, until you are completely fluent.

A word about timing: a key factor in practicing effectively, with number of repetitions kept to the minimum necessary for long-term retention, is how you space your practice sessions. The basic rules are:

- review three times at increasingly spaced intervals
- only successful reviews count
- the spacing should occur just before you are about to forget without review
- as a rule of thumb (since that is tricky to calculate until you've become more familiar with your own learning skills):
  - review for the first time one day after learning
  - 2nd review a week or so later
  - 3rd review a month after that
- it's better to space your reviews longer than too short — make your brain work for it.

Review 1.1

1. What's the mnemonic for remembering the letters that are exactly the same in Russian and English?

   a. KAT

   b. ATOM K

   c. Cat in a Car on Top of the Moon

   d. ATOMIC

2. Match the Russian letters to their associated images.

   M T O C A

3. Pick the Russian letter that corresponds to English letter b:

   a. к

   b. о

   c. б

   d. в

4. Pick the Russian letter that corresponds to English letter c:

   a. к

   b. т

   c. с

   d. х

5. What Russian letters are associated with the following images?

Vocabulary

You only know a few letters so far, so our vocab list is necessarily very short! Don't worry, the lists quickly increase in size, giving you plenty of opportunities for practice.

Here are ten easy Russian words, using the letters you now know:

атом

акт

мама

баба

база

око

бок

оба

тот

так

Some of these words are obvious, others less so (or not at all! — although in general I've avoided including words that have no obvious connections). The collected vocabulary lists in the Glossary include meanings, along with clues to help you remember them. I haven't put those here, because your focus should be on instantly recognizing the letters, and being able to 'read' the words as easily as you do English.

On this first occasion, read the words over as many times as you need, until the letters come fluently — an easy enough task for this first group, but it will get harder with subsequent lists. When you're satisfied with your fluency, check the list with the meanings. Note which words are exactly as expected, and which are not. Read the clues, if any, and see whether they make sense for you — our minds are all different, reflecting our different experiences, so what helps me will not necessarily help you. But my suggestion may spark a different connection for you. Go with it.

When you're learning, and on subsequent reviews, the same 'rule of 3' applies — each word needs to be read easily 3 times.

Note that the fluency you've attained in reading the list the first time is illusory. The words are still fresh in your mind. They haven't yet been transferred to long-term memory. So however easy and obvious they seem, don't forget your reviews. On your reviews, try to read the words for meaning as well.

Spacing your practice

There's a happy line between learning too fast and learning too slow. If you speed through this book too fast, you risk fooling yourself with learning that isn't properly consolidated, and won't necessarily be there when you need it later. You're also more likely to develop confusions between some letters. On the other hand, if you work through the book too slowly, your learning won't feed on itself, and will be much slower (that is, learning will actually be slower, not simply take more time).

At the very end of the book, after the Collected Vocabulary Lists, I have a complete list of the words in alphabetical order. This list doesn't include meanings or transcriptions. It is your final review list. Once you've worked your way through all the letters, use this list for any further reviews.

I suggest you do your first two reviews (at one day and one week) of each list using that list, but use the complete list for your 3rd (and any subsequent) reviews. This will work well if you've got through the lists at a reasonable pace, but if you're slow, you might need to do your 3rd review using the individual lists.

Here's a sample guide to the pace, just to give you the idea:

Day 1: **learn Groups 1 & 2**

Day 2: **review Groups 1 & 2**; **learn Group 3** (assuming you find Groups 1 & 2 easy)

Day 3: if you knew the related Greek letters, you may be ready to **review Group 3**; otherwise, you might need to repeat the learning session

Day 4: if Group 3 review didn't go well, repeat it

Day 5: if all learning has gone well, **learn Group 4**

Day 6: **review Group 4**

Day 7: Group 4 is tricky — even if you did well in the previous review, run through the quick practice to make sure you've got them mastered; if everything is going well, **start learning Group 5**

Day 8: continue learning Group 5

Day 9: **review Groups 1 & 2** (2nd review — remember, only successful reviews count!); **review Group 5** (or continue learning, if necessary)

Day 10: **review Group 3** (2nd review); review Group 5 if you didn't do that yesterday

Day 11: run through the quick practice for Group 5 (assuming the previous review went well)

Day 13: **review Group 4** (2nd review)

Day 14: **start learning Group 6**

Day 15: continue learning Group 6

Day 16: **review Group 5** (2nd review); **review Group 6** (or continue learning, if necessary)

Day 17: run through the quick practice for Group 6 (assuming the previous review went well)

Day 18: **learn Group 7**

Day 19: **review Group 7**

Day 23: **review Group 6** (2nd review)

Day 26: **review Group 7** (2nd review)

Day 56: **complete review** (3rd review)

That all might seem a little over-complicated and intimidating! Don't panic, it's just an illustration, to give you the shape of the process. Note that your learning 'session' might be spread over more than one day, if you're finding a group difficult.

What that means, is that rather than doing a simple review (run through of the vocabulary list), you study the cards again and repeat the test, as well as practicing on the vocab list. You may find it useful to use the 'Quick practice' cards too (you'll see them later, when the letters get more challenging).

You will realize that the early groups inevitably get practiced in the later vocabulary lists; this reduces the need for a formal 3rd review. However, that's not perfect. Once you have all the letters mastered, you can then use the complete list for a 3rd review. You may also feel the need for further reviews.

Individuals vary in their learning abilities in different areas. What's easy for one may be difficult for another. The 'rule of 3' is a guideline. If you remember this type of information easily, you might only need to repeat words twice; if you find this type of learning difficult, you might need to repeat and review four or more times. Moreover, the words themselves make a difference. Easy words, such as the ones in this list, might only need to be covered twice by everyone. The point is to be sensitive to your own learning. Experience will tell you what works for you.

You may find it helpful to use a table like this one (next page), to help you keep track of where you are.

	Review 1	Quick practice	Review 2	Review 3
Groups 1 & 2				
Group 3				
Group 4				
Group 5				
Group 6				
Group 7				
Full list				

Group 3: Greek cousins

Another set of 5 letters will be familiar to those who know the Greek alphabet, or these particular Greek letters anyway: γ, δ, λ, π, φ.

These are all letters that are in relatively common usage, so there's a good chance you know these, even if you're not familiar with the entire Greek alphabet.

Here are the 5 Russian letters based on these:

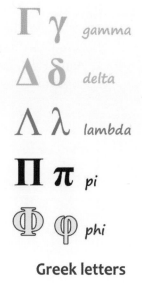

Greek letters

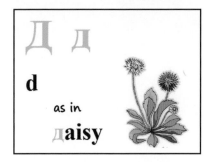

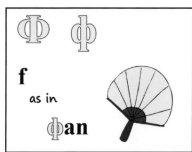

Note the tendency in the Russian alphabet for the lower-case letters to simply be smaller versions of the upper-case letters, rather than distinctly different letters.

Note, too, that while g, p, and f are identical to the Greek upper-case letters, d and l are slightly different. You'll have to make a bit more of an effort to make the connection. I'll talk more about how to do this in a moment. First, for those of you who don't know these Greek letters, here are some mnemonic images to help you remember the novel shapes:

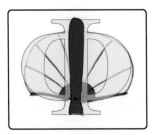

More on practice

Practice recalling your mnemonic images at idle moments such as when you're waiting in line or sitting vacantly on a bus, or resting. I like using the time before I go to sleep, or when I wake during the night, though some may find the activity too stimulating. But this time of day is particularly good for practicing information you want to learn, as it encourages the brain to pay more attention to it, when it's busy processing the day's events during sleep.

Sleep is when the brain chooses which information is worth remembering, and consolidates those memories. So any information or events you run through your mind late in the evening is more likely to be considered worthy, and consolidated (made into a long-term memory).

This is another reason for batching the letters: practice each group in turn, and don't move on until you're confident that you have a reasonable grasp of the letters. They don't have to be totally mastered though, because you'll be reviewing them later, and that's the most important part of the learning process.

You may think that, for that reason, it would be more effective to start with the most difficult letters, and that would be true if it was just a matter of practice effectiveness. But we also have to take into account psychology! Many people would be put off by starting with the most difficult letters, partly because of their difficulty, and partly because they wouldn't have sufficient skill in the learning strategies. Better to get comfortable with the strategies using the easiest letters, which are quickly mastered, and then get into deeper waters.

Time for review

The next group is easier in some ways than the Greek set, but I've put it after to give it more separation from the easy set. You want to have a clear distinction in your mind between this set and the easy set because these are the false friends — those letters that only pretend to look like the letters you're used to.

But before delving into these, check out how well you've mastered the letters we've done so far.

Review 1.2

1. Which of these images represents the Russian letter O?

2. Pick the correct English letter corresponding to the Russian letter represented by this image:

   a. J

   b. G

   c. C

   d. F

3. Which of these images represents the Russian letter A?

4. Pick the correct English letter corresponding to the Russian letter represented by this image:

   a. F

   b. P

   c. O

5. Pick the correct English letter corresponding to the Russian letter represented by this image:

   a. B

   b. O

   c. L

   d. D

6. Which of these images represents the Russian letter T?

7. Which of these images represents the Russian letter M?

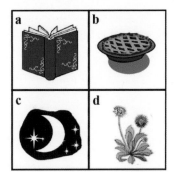

8. Pick the correct English letter corresponding to the Russian letter represented by this image:

   a. P

   b. N

   c. M

   d. T

9. Pick the correct English letter corresponding to the Russian letter represented by this image:

   a. T

   b. L

   c. D

   d. A

10. Which of these images represents the Russian letter K?

Vocabulary

Here are 15 Russian words to practice on:

догма

лог

факт

папа

дама

дом

под

глаз

зал

мозг

пол

бог

год

пока

мало

Group 4: False friends

These 6 letters are all identical to letters in our alphabet, but they are not the letters you think they are! So note the pronunciations carefully, and use the images to help you remember them.

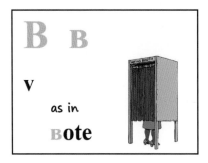

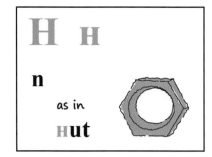

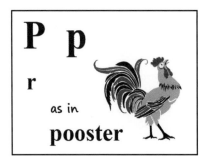

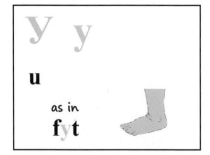

Note the tricky pronunciation of X — this doesn't correspond to an English letter, but is familiar from the hard kh / ch sound used in Scottish loch, or the German composer Bach.

Here's a mnemonic to help you remember which letters are in this set of false friends: **CHuBbY PiXie**.

We've covered half the letters in the Russian alphabet now — the easy half, largely. Before delving into deeper waters, do make sure that you've got a solid grasp of the letters so far. To help you with that, here they are all together:

Review 1.3

1. Pick the English letter that corresponds to Russian letter Л:

    a. P

    b. D

    c. L

    d. N

2. For the following images, pick the Russian letter associated with them:

А Д З М Н Р

3. Pick the English letter that corresponds to Russian letter Г:

    a. L

    b. G

    c. F

    d. T

4. For the following images, pick the Russian letter associated with them:

Б Г О С Т Ф

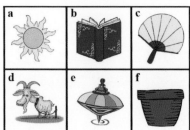

5. Pick the English letter that corresponds to Russian letter Н:

   a. H
   b. P
   c. B
   d. N

6. Pick the English letter that corresponds to Russian letter Ф:

   a. F
   b. P
   c. C
   d. O

7. Pick the English letter that corresponds to Russian letter Р:

   a. N
   b. R
   c. P
   d. F

8. For the following images, pick the Russian letter associated
   with them:

В   К   Л   П   У   Х
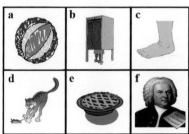

9. Pick the English letter that corresponds to Russian letter C:

    a. C

    b. K

    c. X

    d. S

10. Pick the English letter that corresponds to Russian letter Д:

    a. L

    b. N

    c. I

    d. D

11. Pick the English letter that corresponds to Russian letter B:

    a. F

    b. P

    c. V

    d. B

12. Pick the English letter that corresponds to Russian letter П:

    a. N

    b. D

    c. P

    d. M

13. Pick the English letter that corresponds to Russian letter У:

    a. W

    b. U

    c. Y

    d. I

14. Pick the English letter that corresponds to Russian letter X:

    a. K

    b. X

    c. KH

    d. C

15. Pick the English letter that corresponds to Russian letter З:

    a. E

    b. Z

    c. A

    d. T

Vocabulary

We now have enough letters to create a lot of words. This means we can have several lists, so that you can practice and review using different sets of words. Just use the first list on your initial learning session.

List 1

август	логос
вагон	магнат
Москва	оратор
норма	волк
адвокат	мантра
команда	нота
арка	матрона
фронт	банк
брат	нос
вода	орган
водка	парабола
доктор	фактор
карта	

List 2

солдат

капсула

фантом

лакуна

фонд

гуру

аура

фортуна

корпус

луна

монумент

натура

опус

курс

оракул

форум

постулат

правда

работа

класс

план

статус

форма

роман

пара

List 3

сам	ступор
два	зуб
конклав	рота
гумус	друг
корпускула	ухо
автор	сон
колонна	окно
сумма	он
ход	сто
квадрат	город
фабула	стол
арматура	страх
остров	

Quick practice

Use these cards to quickly practice these tricky letters. The mnemonic image reminds you of the sound of the letter and its transcription — you want to build a strong link between this image and the Russian letter, so that when you see, for example, an н, you automatically think of the nut, and from there, connect it to English n.

To practice these, then, you simply look at the card, and say to yourself: "nut, n", "rooster, r", "vote, v", etc. Your aim is to practice this (over time) until your responses are reliably automatic — which means that no thought is required.

Now, I know it will be tempting to cut out the additional step of remembering the object — why not simply look at the н, and say n? But the object image has much greater memorability. Including it will create a more durable memory, and it will be easier to remember.

Group 5: Tricky vowels

The tricky thing about vowels is that we (English speakers) think there are only 5, but that's because we don't distinguish (in writing) the sound differences that we make. So, you'll have noticed that in the first set we had 'a' pronounced as in 'car' or 'father' (that's the traditional example, but car is easier to picture!), and 'o' as in 'pot'. The former is long, and the latter is short. The other variants aren't used in Russian, but as you'll see, they do have their own variants to make up for it.

Here are the first two:

Pay careful attention to the similarities and differences between these vowels. In the first pair, for example, the two represent long (ee) and short (the i sound at the end of boy) versions of i.

Note too, the vowels that are pronounced with an initial 'y' sound. Use the pictures to help you remember the pronunciation.

Pay careful attention to how this letter differs from the letter for z:

З з

And now the 'y' set (4 members):

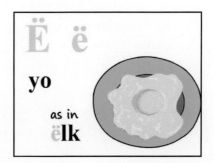

Most of these shapes aren't that unfamiliar. Indeed, ye is identical to English e, and yo just needs an additional two dots. So for these, you simply need to pay attention to this difference. You may find it helps to think of as the dots as tiny yolks.

Four of the other letters are reversals of English letters:

- i and y are backwards Ns (to remember which has the small curved dash, think of the boy having a cap)

- e is a backward E, of a sort — or it may be more helpful to realize it's the same as the symbol for the euro

- ya is a backwards R.

The only really novel letter, then, is yu, which very closely resembles IO. You might find it useful, therefore, to use the mnemonic **IOU** to help you remember this Russian letter.

Review 1.4

1. For the following images, pick the Russian letter associated with them:

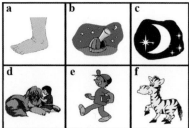

М З Э У Ю Й

2. What's the mnemonic for remembering the letters that are "false friends"?

   a. ATOM K

   b. Atomic Kat

   c. CHuBbY PiXie

   d. GoDoLPHin

3. Which of these images represents the Russian letter Е?

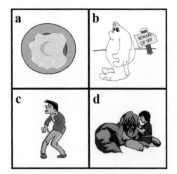

4. Pick the English letter that corresponds to Russian letter Ю:

   a. o

   b. ye

   c. yo

   d. yu

5. For the following images, pick the Russian letter associated with them:

Л В Н Я П И

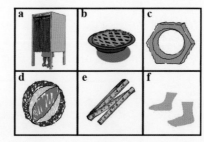

6. Pick the Russian letter that corresponds to English letter e:

   a. З

   b. Е

   c. Э

   d. Ё

7. Pick the English letter that corresponds to Russian letter Я:

   a. r

   b. yu

   c. ya

   d. p

8. Pick the English letter that corresponds to Russian letter Ё:

   a. e

   b. oi

   c. ye

   d. yo

9. Which of these images represents the Russian letter Ё?

10. Pick the Russian letter that corresponds to English letter i:

    a. Й

    b. Ё

    c. У

    d. И

11. Pick the Russian letter that corresponds to English letter y:

    a. Й

    b. И

    c. У

    d. Ю

12. What Russian letters would you use for the underlined sounds: one f<u>oo</u>t, two f<u>ee</u>t?

    a. О, Е

    b. О, Й

    c. У, И

    d. У, Й

Vocabulary

List 1

телефон

актёр

вентилятор

гармония

статуя

базис

аспект

дебитор

библиотека

диктатор

идол

декада

институт

коллега

индустрия

амброзия

кредит

демократия

легион

экстенсия

магнитуда

иммунитет

спина

мастер

инструктор

List 2

медиатор

конфессия

мембрана

этнос

гемма

индекс

мне

территория

эон

монитор

навигация

инструмент

один

дивизион

синопсис

плутократия

три

привилегия

спектр

материя

континент

проблема

нотариус

энергия

фундамент

List 3

интеллект

метр

профессия

администратор

профессор

радикал

документ

эдикт

республика

эксперимент

сегмент

интервал

опера

пигмент

текст

сектор

доктрина

проспект

идея

министр

студия

радиус

архитектор

суспензия

публика

List 4

вилла	характер
теория	центурия
идиот	аудитория
трансфузия	цилиндр
сестра	сенатор
история	чемпион
фамилия	экзамен
ордер	вино
аудитор	агитатор
фантазия	эксперт
элемент	гиппопотам
фигура	эффект
секрет	

Quick practice

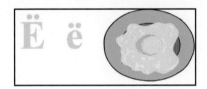

Group 6: Novel letters

There are only a few letters in the Russian alphabet that are completely new to an English speaker. These all represent sounds that have no direct equivalent in English, but even their shapes are mostly not that outlandish, as you can see. For example, let's start with these three letters, which, as you can see, resemble the Roman characters for 2 and 3.

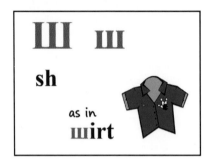

How to remember these novel letters? First of all, of course, we note their similarity to Roman numbers 2 and 3, and take careful note of the similarities and differences. The two letters similar to the Roman 3 both represent the sound sh, but the sheep sh is a softer sound (say the words shirt and sheep and you'll hear the subtle difference). You could help yourself remember that it's the softer sh that has that little tail on it by thinking that sheep poop, unlike shirts.

Note that the ts letter, which resembles the Roman 2, also has that tail.

How to remember that the sh letters have 3 columns, while ts has only 2? You could try the mnemonic: 2 bats, 3 sheep. See how, in the picture, two sheep have a bat to play with, but the 3rd sheep, sadly, is left out. Think of that sad sheep.

Another image may also help you build this connection between ts and the 2

upright pillars of the letter. See how, in this image, a ball has knocked out one wicket, leaving only 2 upright. Notice how the bail on top of the wickets has gone flying, leaving them open at top. Notice the green grass they're standing on, providing a firm base. See how one bat leans agains the 2nd wicket, providing the 'tail'.

The 4th letter in this group is also not so unfamiliar — see how the letter for the sound ch resembles a rotated h (which is especially useful, since h is part of the ch transliteration.

You may also find it helpful to note its resemblance to a candelabra, which fits with the idea of a church.

The final letter in the set is a completely novel shape, and an unfamiliar letter combination, although the sound does exist in English. The zh sound is found in pleasure, or leisure. Both are appropriate for the image I have used.

Pay careful attention to how the image can be mapped onto the letter.

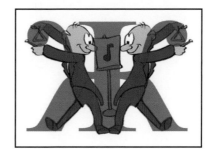

Review 1.5

1. For the following images, pick the Russian letter associated with them

А К Л П Т Г

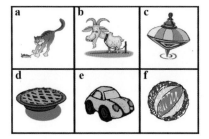

2. Which of these images represents the Russian letter Ч?

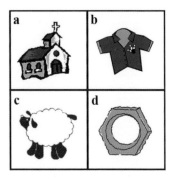

3. For the following images, pick the Russian letter associated with them:

В Р С Х З А

4. Which of these images represents the Russian letter Ш?

5. For the following images, pick the Russian letter associated with them:

Ф У Б Н О Д

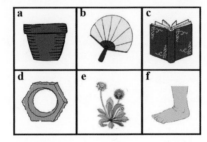

6. Which of these images represents the Russian letter Ц?

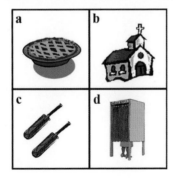

7. Pick the English letter that corresponds to Russian letter Ш:

    a. ts

    b. ch

    c. sh

    d. zh

8. Pick the Russian letter that corresponds to English letter-combination ts:

    a. Щ

    b. С

    c. Ц

    d. Ж

9. Pick the English letter that corresponds to Russian letter Ж:

    a. zh

    b. sh

    c. kh

    d. x

10. Pick the English letter that corresponds to Russian letter Щ:

    a. ts

    b. zh

    c. wh

    d. sh

11. Pick the Russian letter that corresponds to English letter-combination zh:

    a. Ж

    b. Ш

    c. Щ

    d. Ч

12. Pick the Russian letter that corresponds to English letter-combination ch:

a. У

b. Ш

c. Н

d. Ч

Vocabulary

List 1

вентиляция

декламация

импликация

коллекция

щека

лекция

экзекуция

матрица

деменция

луч

апокалипсис

модификация

нация

конструкция

инвенция

аппетит

номинация

администрация

чай

товарищ

List 2

инициация

обструкция

ситуация

что

машина

субдукция

прокламация

оппозиция

аппендикс

медицина

конституция

верификация

оккупация

интерпозиция

бабушка

компенсация

патриций

ящик

демонстрация

нотация

List 3

ассимиляция

конфирмация

революция

интенция

потенция

конвенция

рекламация

нумерация

популяция

аукцион

ротация

ключ

принц

спекуляция

деструкция

щит

эссенция

комбинация

инструкция

традиция

List 4

ассигнация

репрезентация

концепция

час

жена

редукция

трансляция

флуктуация

кондиция

дистанция

следующий

фортификация

ретенция

школа

эволюция

интеллигенция

провинция

юстиция

офицер

информация

Quick practice

Group 7: The little b set

Finally, we have a very curious trio, with no equivalence in English.

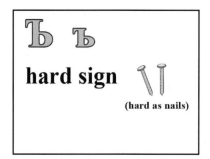

This small set have more in common than their shape. There's also the matter of their English equivalence.

The first two aren't pronounced at all — they appear when it's necessary to indicate that the preceding letter is pronounced 'hard' or 'soft'. Note the difference between the two shapes, which is quite subtle: the hard sign has an elongated top.

The 3rd 'little b' makes a sound that doesn't appear in English. It's transcribed as a y, and might be thought of as a 'hard' i. That gives us 3 letters that correspond to an i / y: И, Й, and Ы.

Note, too, the other letters that are 'b's: Б б, and В в. Particularly with the first of these, study the differences between them carefully, so you don't confuse them.

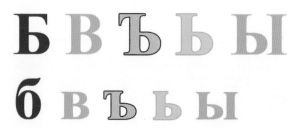

Review 1.6

1. For the following images, pick the Russian letter associated with them:

У Ч Щ Э Я Й

2. Which of these images represents the Russian letter Ь?

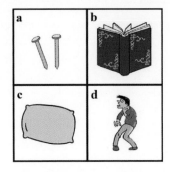

3. For the following images, pick the Russian letter associated with them:

Е Ё Ю Ц Ш Ж

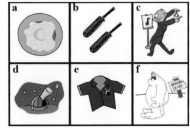

4. Pick the English letter that corresponds to Russian letter Б:

   a. v

   b. d

   c. b

   d. no corresponding sound

5. Which of these images represents the Russian letter Ъ?

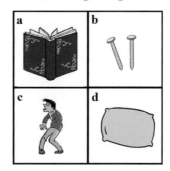

6. Which of these images represents the Russian letter Ы?

7. Pick the English letter that corresponds to Russian letter Ъ:

    a. b

    b. i

    c. y

    d. no corresponding sound

8. Pick the Russian letter that transliterates as y in English:

    a. Ы

    b. И

    c. Й

    d. У

9. Pick the English letter that corresponds to Russian letter Ь:

    a. i

    b. b

    c. u

    d. no corresponding sound

10. Which of these Russian letters signifies that the preceding letter is pronounced as its hard variant?

    a. Ь

    b. Ъ

    c. Б

    d. Ы

11. Which of these Russian letters signifies that the preceding letter is pronounced as its soft variant?

    a. Ъ

    b. Ы

    c. Ь

    d. Б

12. For the following Russian letters, pick the English letters or letter combinations associated with them:

yo e i ye y

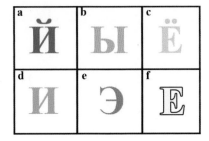

Vocabulary

List 1

анонимный

госпиталь

декабрь

капитель

мать

нормальный

объект

гость

продуктивный

секретарь

модуль

артикль

солидный

демонстрировать

календарь

сын

новый

текстиль

культура

территориальный

List 2

мы

экскременты

день

ночь

путь

четыре

любовь

камень

результат

бутылка

шесть

рубль

съезд

дочь

пять

опыт

десятьп

выход

музыка

король

List 3

дым	сечь
соль	вещь
объяснить	небольшой
большой	семь
тридцать	роль
целый	вечный
странный	печь
холодный	слабый
быть	данный
площадь	жечь

Quick practice

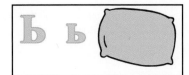 

Learning the alphabet

Now that you know the letters, it's time to consolidate them into the alphabet, and learn their order — vital if you're to look words up in a dictionary, and also useful for cementing them into your long-term memory. This is partly because it gives you other connections and potential retrieval cues, and also because it will provide another way of practicing your letters.

Although we're learning them in alphabetical order, we won't try and grasp them right away as one long chain. Once again, we'll chunk them.

Here are the first 8 letters with the English transliteration.

How to remember this order? You could try repeating the English transliterations over and over, while looking at the Russian letters. This is the default strategy of most students, and I mention it so I can clearly and explicitly say: this is not a good strategy!

A decidedly better step would be to write the Russian letters as you repeat the English transliterations, but this is still far from the best strategy (although writing the Russian letters is itself a good thing to do). This sort of situation — remembering the order of things — is exactly what list mnemonics were designed to help with.

On the next page you will also see a visually enhanced mnemonic story, with associated images, to help you. This image of the text is to re-emphasize the visual aspect from the cards, but here is the 'story' in a more readable format:

> The **car** drove over the **book** in its zeal to **vote**, but the **goat** was more interested in the **daisy**, though the **yeti** thought an egg **yolk** would give more **pleasure**.

А	а	**a**
Б	б	**b**
В	в	**v**
Г	г	**g**
Д	д	**d**
Е	е	**ye**
Ё	ё	**yo**
Ж	ж	zh

the **car** drove over the
book in its zeal to
вote but the
гoat was more interested
in the **дaisy** though the
ⓔti thought an egg **ёlk**
would give more **pleaжure**

Now I know, if you haven't used this sort of mnemonic before, it's going to seem daft to you, and you won't believe it's really going to help! But do try; I do assure you that this sort of strategy is of proven effectiveness. You really will be surprised how much easier such nonsensical stories are to remember than a list of words, or, worse, a list of letters. (If you want to come up with your own story based on these words, in this order, feel free! if you've created it yourself, it will probably work better.)

So what do you do with this story? Rather than repeating letters while picturing the Russian letters, repeat the story while visualizing the images. Yes, you still need some repetition, but you'll find you need far less than you would for less memorable information. Once you have the story firmly fixed in your head, visualize the Russian letters as you say each keyword.

When you're confident you've got this first story in your head, you can move on to the next 8 letters.

З з	**з**	**z**
И и	**и**	**i**
Й й	**й**	**y**
К к	**к**	**c**
Л л	**л**	**l**
М м	**м**	**m**
Н н	**н**	**n**
О о	**о**	**o**

The **zebra** stomped on the **feet** of the **boy** running from the **cat** scared of the **ball** under a **moon** where a **nut** could break a **pot**.

the **Зebra** *stomped on the* **fиt** *of the* **boй** *running from the* **кat** *scared of the* **baлл** *under a* **moon** *where a* **нut** *could break a* **pot**

The trick to mastering these stories is to really think about each link: the zebra stomping on the feet; the feet of the boy being horrifyingly separated from him; the boy fleeing from the scared cat; the cat fleeing from the large ball.

Pay particular attention to the weaker connections in the story, such as the ball under the moon. You can elaborate these if necessary, such as visualizing the 'horn' of the crescent moon puncturing the beach ball.

Once you've got that story fixed in your mind, remind yourself of the first set, then, when you're confident you've got both sets mastered, move on to the 3rd set (9 letters).

Pie pecked by a **rooster** and cooked by the **sun** that spins the **top** into the **foot** can be cooled by his **fan** if **Bach** would stop throwing **bats** at the **church**.

пie pecked by a **pooster** and cooked by the **cun** that spins the тop into the **f**y**t** can be cooled by his фan if **Ba**x would stop throwing **ba**ц at the чиrч

The connection between foot and fan is perhaps the weakest in this story. It may help to remember that both begin with f. Additional information such as this can strengthen the connection. Don't worry about overloading with too much information (within reason!) — this is much less of a concern when the information is part of an integrated cluster.

In the same way — did you notice how I mentioned how many letters were in each set? Each set has 8 letters, except the 3rd, which has 9. The reason why you should take note of this information is that it provides an

П	п	p
Р	р	r
С	с	s
Т	т	t
У	у	u
Ф	ф	f
Х	х	kh
Ц	ц	ts
Ч	ч	ch

additional memory help, so that you can check you've remembered all the letters in the set (and haven't 'over-remembered' — putting in additional letters that don't belong). You don't need to make a big effort to remember this sort of information, just pay attention to it, and use it (say, by checking each letter off on your fingers). A few occasions of this will see the information naturally attach.

Here's the final set of 8 letters, and its mnemonic story:

A **shirt** for a **sheep** is one thing, but it's hard and a little **disgusting** to be so **soft** on a **pet** when the **universe** is our **yardstick**.

Ш	Ш	sh
Щ	Щ	sh
Ъ	Ъ	
Ы	ы	y
Ь	ь	
Э	э	e
Ю	ю	yu
Я	я	ya

a **ш**irt for a **щ**еер

is one thing, but it's hard **Ъ**

and a little disgusting **ы** (ih)

to be so soft **ь** on a р**э**t

when the **ю**niverse

is our **я**rdstick

Once you've mastered the 4 mnemonic stories, you'll realize there's some other obvious weak connections — namely, those between each set. How do you remember which set follows which? Here are 3 brief phrase-pictures to help with this.

And here's the complete alphabet, all in one place:

the pleaжure of a Зebra

pot пie

not a чигч шirt!

А а	a
Б б	b
В в	v
Г г	g
Д д	d
Е е	ye
Ё ё	yo
Ж ж	zh
З з	z
И и	i
Й й	y
К к	c
Л л	l
М м	m
Н н	n
О о	o
П п	p
Р р	r
С с	s
Т т	t
У у	u
Ф ф	f
Х х	kh
Ц ц	ts
Ч ч	ch
Ш ш	sh
Щ щ	sh
Ъ ъ	
Ы ы	y
Ь ь	
Э э	e
Ю ю	yu
Я я	ya

Complete Review List

Use this list for any later reviews once you've worked through the book. This complete list is in alphabetical order, so you can also use this, if you wish, to quickly check whether any specific word is included.

август	аудитор
автор	аудитория
агитатор	аукцион
адвокат	аура
администратор	баба
администрация	бабушка
акт	база
актёр	базис
амброзия	банк
анонимный	библиотека
апокалипсис	бог
аппендикс	бок
аппетит	большой
арка	брат
арматура	бутылка
артикль	быть
архитектор	вагон
аспект	вентилятор
ассигнация	вентиляция
ассимиляция	верификация
атом	вечный

вещь

вилла

вино

вода

водка

волк

выход

гармония

гемма

гиппопотам

глаз

год

город

госпиталь

гость

гумус

гуру

дама

данный

два

дебитор

декабрь

декада

декламация

деменция

демократия

демонстрация

демонстрировать

день

деструкция

десять

дивизион

диктатор

дистанция

догма

доктор

доктрина

документ

дом

дочь

друг

дым

жена

жечь

зал

зуб

идея

идиот

идол

иммунитет

импликация

инвенция

индекс

индустрия

инициация

институт

инструктор

инструкция

инструмент

интеллект

интеллигенция

интенция

интервал

интерпозиция

информация

история

календарь

камень

капитель

капсула

карта

квадрат

класс

ключ

коллега

коллекция

колонна

команда

комбинация

компенсация

конвенция

кондиция

конклав

конституция

конструкция

континент

конфессия

конфирмация

концепция

король

корпус

корпускула

кредит

культура

курс

лакуна

легион

лекция

лог

логос

луна

луч

любовь

магнат

магнитуда

мало

мама

мантра

мастер

материя

матрица

матрона

мать

машина

медиатор

медицина

мембрана

метр

министр

мне

модификация

модуль

мозг

монитор

монумент

Москва

музыка

мы

навигация

натура

нация

небольшой

новый

номинация

норма

нормальный

нос

нота

нотариус

нотация

ночь

нумерация

оба

обструкция

объект

объяснить

один

оккупация

окно

око

он

опера

оппозиция

опус

опыт

оракул

оратор

орган

ордер

остров

офицер

папа

пара

парабола

патриций

печь

пигмент

план

площадь

плутократия

под

пока

пол

популяция

постулат

потенция

правда

привилегия

принц

проблема

провинция

продуктивный

прокламация

проспект

профессия

профессор

публика

путь

пять

работа

радикал

радиус

революция

редукция

результат

рекламация

репрезентация

республика

ретенция

роль

роман

рота

ротация

рубль

сам

сегмент

секрет

секретарь

сектор

семь

сенатор

сестра

сечь

синопсис

ситуация

слабый

следующий

солдат

солидный

соль

сон

спектр

спекуляция

спина

статус

статуя

сто

стол

странный

страх

студия

ступор

субдукция

сумма

суспензия

съезд

сын

так

текст

текстиль

телефон

теория

территориальный

территория

товарищ

тот

традиция

трансляция

трансфузия

три

тридцать

ухо

фабула

факт

фактор

фамилия

фантазия

фантом

фигура

флуктуация

фонд

форма

фортификация

фортуна

форум

фронт

фундамент

характер

ход

холодный

целый

центурия

цилиндр

чай

час

чемпион

четыре

что

шесть

школа

щека

щит

эволюция

эдикт

экзамен

экзекуция

экскременты

эксперимент

эксперт

экстенсия

элемент

энергия

эон

эссенция

этнос

эффект

юстиция

ящик

Answers to review questions

Review 1.1

1. b
2. (a) О   (b) А   (c) Т   (d) К   (e) М
3. c
4. a
5. (a) З   (b) Б

Review 1.2

1. c
2. b
3. d
4. a
5. c
6. a
7. c
8. a
9. c
10. b

Review 1.3

1. c
2. (a) М   (b) Д   (c) Н   (d) Р   (e) а   (f) З
3. b

4. (a) С (b) Б (c) Ф (d) Г (e) Т (f) О
5. d
6. a
7. b
8. (a) Л (b) В (c) У (d) К (e) П (f) Х
9. d
10. d
11. c
12. c
13. b
14. c
15. b

Review 1.4

1. (a) У (b) Ю (c) М (d) Э (e) Й (f) З
2. c
3. b
4. d
5. (a) В (b) П (c) Н (d) Л (e) Я (f) И
6. a
7. c
8. d
9. b
10. d
11. a
12. c

Review 1.5

1. (a) К (b) Г (c) Т (d) П (e) А (f) Л
2. a
3. (a) С (b) Х (c) В (d) Р (e) А (f) З
4. b
5. (a) О (b) Ф (c) Б (d) Н (e) Д (f) У
6. c
7. c
8. c
9. a
10. d
11. a
12. d

Review 1.6

1. (a) Я (b) Э (c) Щ (d) У (e) Ч (f) Й
2. c
3. (a) Ё (b) Ц (c) Ж (d) Ю (e) Ш (f) Е
4. b
5. c
6. b
7. d
8. c
9. d
10. b
11. c
12. (a) y (b) y (c) yo (d) i (e) e (f) ye

Glossary

Words chosen have been taken either from my Indo-European Cognate Dictionary, or from a list of the 1000 most frequent Russian words. They have been chosen either because of their close similarity to their English counterparts, or because their cognate relationship offers a hook for remembering ('cognate' means the Russian and English words ultimately have the same ancestor), or in some cases, because the word is common and a mnemonic is reasonably obvious.

Vocabulary for Groups 1 & 2

атом (atom), atom

акт (act), act

мама (mama), mummy

баба (baba), woman, wife, old woman — easy if you've heard of the fairy-tale witch Baba Yaga

база (baza), base

око (oko), eye (dated/poetic) — cognate with ocular and oculist

бок (bok), side, flank — think of a book on its side

оба (oba), both — cognate with ambi-, as in ambidextrous

тот (tot), that — That's a tot

так (tak), so, then — Take it then

Vocabulary for Group 3

догма (dogma), dogma

лог (log), ravine — The log rolls down the ravine

факт (fact), fact

папа (papa), Papa, daddy

дама (dama), lady, dance-partner, queen in cards — cognate with dame

дом (dom), home, house — cognate with domestic

под (pod), under — cognate with foot, think of something being underfoot

глаз (glaz), eye, eyesight — think of a glass eye, or an eye glazing over

зал (zal), hall, room — cognate with the French word salle

мозг (mozg), brain, bone marrow — cognate with marrow, It's like a mosquito in my brain

пол (pol), floor, gender — Polish the floor, is Pol a boy or girl?

бог (bog), god, idol — The god is bog, The bog is full of idols

год (god), year — cognate with good, think of a good year

пока (poka), for now — Let's polka for now, Let's play poker for now

мало (malo), little, few — Only a little mail! So few males

Vocabulary for Group 4

List 1

август (avgust), August

вагон (vagon), railway carriage, coach — cognate with wagon

Москва (Moskva), Moscow

норма (norma), norm, standard

адвокат (advokat), lawyer, advocate

команда (komanda), team, command

арка (arka), arch, arc

фронт (front), front

брат (brat), brother — cognate, My brother is a brat

вода (voda), water — cognates

водка (vodka), vodka

доктор (doktor), doctor

карта (karta), map, chart

логос (logos), logos

магнат (magnat), magnate, tycoon

оратор (orator), orator

волк (volk), wolf — cognates

мантра (mantra), mantra

нота (nota), note

матрона (matrona), matron

банк (bank), bank

нос (nos), nose — cognate

орган (organ), organ

парабола (parabola), parabola

фактор (faktor), factor

List 2

солдат (soldat), soldier — cognate

капсула (kapsula), capsule

фантом (fantom), phantom

лакуна (lakuna), lacuna

фонд (fond), fund

гуру (guru), guru

аура (aura), aura

фортуна (fortuna), fortune

корпус (korpus), body — cognate with corpus and corpse

луна (luna), moon — cognate with lunar

монумент (monument), monument

натура (natura), nature

опус (opus), opus

курс (kurs), course

оракул (orakul), oracle

форум (forum), forum

постулат (postulat), postulate

правда (pravda), truth — the name of a famous Russian newspaper

работа (rabota), work, job — cognate with robot, A job for a robot

класс (klass), class)

план (plan), plan

статус (status), status

форма (forma), form, shape, uniform

роман (roman), novel, romance — from French roman

пара (para), pair — cognates

List 3

сам (sam), self — cognate with same

два (dva), 2 — cognate with twin, and French deux

конклав (konklav), conclave

гумус (gumus), humus

корпускула (korpuskula), corpuscle

автор (avtor), author

колонна (kolonna), column

сумма (summa), sum, amount

ход (khod), motion, movement — cognate with hodo- in hodometer, an old form of odometer, The movement of cod

квадрат (kvadrat), square, quadrate

фабула (fabula), story — cognate with fable

арматура (armatura), armature

остров (ostrov), island — cognate with stream, A (o) stream (strov) around the island

ступор (stupor), stupor

зуб (zub), tooth — cognates

рота (rota), military company — The company is next on the rota

друг (drug), close friend — a friend is like a drug

ухо (ukho), ear — cognates, also with aural, An ear is like a hook

сон (son), sleep, dream — cognate with somnolent, My son is in a dream

окно (okno), window — from око, meaning eye

он (on), he, it — He is on it

сто (sto), 100 — cognate with cent

город (gorod), city, town — cognate with garden and yard, Garden City

стол (stol), table — cognate with stool, A stool at the table

страх (strax), fear — Struck with fear

Vocabulary for Group 5

List 1

телефон (telefon), telephone

актёр (aktyor), actor

вентиля́тор (ventilyator), fan — ventilator

гармония (garmoniya), harmony

статуя (statuya), statue

базис (bazis), basis

аспект (aspekt), aspect

дебитор (debitor), debtor

библиотека (biblioteka), library — cognate with French bibliothèque диктатор (diktator), dictator

идол (idol), idol

декада (dekada), decade

институт (institut), institute

коллега (kollega), colleague

индустрия (industriya), industry

амброзия (ambroziya), ambrosia

кредит (kredit), credit

демократия (demokratiya), democracy

легион (legion), legion

экстенсия (ekstenciya), extensionality

магнитуда (magnituda), magnitude

иммунитет (immunitet), immunity

спина (spina), back — cognate with spine

мастер (master), master

инструктор (instruktor), instructor

List 2

медиатор (mediator), mediator

конфессия (konfessiya), confession

мембрана (membrana), membrane

этнос (etnos), ethnos

гемма (gemma), gem

индекс (indeks), index

мне (mne), to me

территория (territoriya), territory

эон (eon), eon/aeon

монитор (monitor), monitor

навигация (navigatsiya), navigation

инструмент (instrument), instrument

один (odin), one — Odin the one-eyed

дивизион (divizion), division

синопсис (sinopsis), synopsis

плутократия (plutokratiya), plutocracy

три (tri), three

привилегия (privilegiya), privilege

спектр (spektr), spectrum

материя (materiya), matter

континент (kontinent), continent

проблема (problema), problem

нотариус (notarius), notary

энергия (energiya), energy

фундамент (fundament), foundation — fundamental

List 3

интеллект (intellekt), intelligence, intellect

метр (metr), meter/metre

профессия (professiya), profession

администратор (administrator), administrator

профессор (professor), professor

радикал (radikal), radical

документ (dokument), document

эдикт (edikt), edict

республика (respublika), republic

эксперимент (exsperiment), experiment

сегмент (segment), segment

интервал (interval), interval

опера (opera), opera

пигмент (pigment), pigment

текст (tekst), text

сектор (sektor), sector

доктрина (doktrina), doctrine

проспект (prospekt), avenue — cognate with prospect

идея (ideya), idea

министр (ministr), minister

студия (studiya), studio

радиус (radius), radius

архитектор (arkhitektor), architect

суспензия (suspenziya), suspension

публика (publika), public

List 4

вилла (villa), villa

теория (teoriya), theory

идиот (idiot), idiot

трансфузия (transfuziya), transfusion

сестра (sestra), sister

история (istoriya), history

фамилия (familiya), surname — family name

ордер (order), order

аудитор (auditor), auditor

фантазия (fantziya), fantasy

элемент (element), element

фигура (figura), figure

секрет (sekret), secret

характер (kharakter), character

центурия (tsenturiya), century

аудитория (auditoriya), auditorium

цилиндр (tsilindr), cylinder

сенатор (senator), senator

чемпион (chempion), champion

экзамен (ekzamen), exam

вино (vino), wine

агитатор (agitator), agitator

эксперт (ekspert), expert

гиппопотам (gippopotam), hippopotamus

эффект (effekt), effect

Vocabulary for Group 6

List 1

вентиляция (ventilyatsiya), ventilation

декламация (deklamatsiya), recitation — declamation

импликация (implikatsiya), implication

коллекция (kollektsiya), collection

щека(sheka), cheek

лекция (lektsiya), lecture

экзекуция (ekzekutsiya), execution

матрица (matritsa), matrix

деменция (dementsiya), dementia

луч (luč), ray, beam — cognate with lux and light

апокалипсис (apokalipsis), apocalypse

модификация (modifikatsiya), modification

нация (natsiya), nation

конструкция (konstruktsiya), construction, design

инвенция (inventsiya), inventory

аппетит (appetit), appetite

номинация (nominatsiya), nomination

администрация (administratsiya), administration

чай (chai), tea

товарищ(tovarish), friend

List 2

инициация (initsiatsiya), initiation

обструкция (obstruktsiya), obstruction

ситуация (situatsiya), situation

что (što), what — So what?

машина (mashina), machine, car, engine

субдукция (subduktsiya), subduction

прокламация (proklamatsiy), proclamation

оппозиция (oppozitsiya), opposition

аппендикс (appendiks), appendix

медицина (meditsina), medicine

конституция (konstitutsiya), constitution

верификация (verifikatsiya), verification

оккупация (okkupatsiya), occupation

интерпозиция (interpozitsiya), interposition

бабушка (babushka), grandmother

компенсация (kompensatsiya), compensation

патриций (patritsiy), patrician

ящик(yashik), box, case — cognate with ash, meaning the tree

демонстрация (demonstratsiya), demonstration

нотация (notatsiya), notation

List 3

ассимиляция (assimilyatsiya), assimilation

конфирмация (konfirmatsiya), confirmation

революция (revolyutsiya), revolution

интенция (intentsiya), intention, intent

потенция (potentsiya), potency

конвенция (konventsiya), convention

рекламация (reklamatsiya), reclamation

нумерация (numeratsiya), numbering, enumeration

популяция (populyatsiya), population

аукцион (auktsion), auction

ротация (rotatsiya), rotation

ключ (ključ), key, clue

принц (prints), prince

спекуляция (spekulyatsiya), speculation

деструкция (destruktsiya), destruction

щит (ščit), shield — cognate with scutum, but this is not a common word, however shield itself is quite similar, if you think about it

эссенция (eccentsiya), essence

комбинация (kombinatsiya), combination

инструкция (instruktsiya), instruction, manual

традиция (traditsiya), tradition

List 4

ассигнация (assignatsiya), banknote (dated), payment order — cognate with assignation

репрезентация (reprezentatsiya), representation

концепция (kontseptsiya), concept

час (chas), hour, time — Just an hour

жена (zhena), wife — cognate with queen

редукция (reduktsiya), reduction

трансляция (translyatsiya), broadcast, transmission, translation

флуктуация (fluktuatsiya), fluctuation

кондиция (konditsiya), condition

дистанция (distantsiya), distance

следующий (sleduyushiy), next, following — It's next on the schedule

фортификация (fortifikatsiya), fortification

ретенция (retentsiya), retention

школа (shkola), school

эволюция (evolyutsiya), evolution

интеллигенция (intelligentsiya), intelligentsia

провинция (provintsiya), province

юстиция (yustitsiya), justice

офицер (ofitser), officer

информация (informatsiya), information

Vocabulary for Group 7

List 1

анонимный (anonimnyy), anonymous

госпиталь (gospital'), hospital

декабрь (dekabr'), December

капитель (kapitel'), capital

мать (mat'), mother

нормальный (normal'nyy), normal

объект (ob''jekt), object

гость (gost'), guest

продуктивный (produktivnyy), productive

секретарь (sekretar'), secretary

модуль (modul'), module

артикль (artikl'), article

солидный (solidnyy), solid

демонстрировать (demonstrirovat'), demonstrate

календарь (kalendar'), calendar

сын (syn), son

новый (novyy), new — cognate with novel, and new

текстиль (tekstil'), textile

культура (kul'tura), culture

территориальный (territorial'nyy), territorial

List 2

мы (my), we, me

экскременты (ekskrementy), excrement

день (den'), day — cognates

ночь (noch'), night — cognates

путь (put'), way, path — cognate with path, Put me on the path

четыре (chetyre), four — cognate with tetra-, as in tetrapod, and quadra-, as in quadraped and quadrangle

любовь (lyubov'), love — cognates

камень (kamen'), stone — cognate with hammer

результат (resul'tat), result, outcome

бутылка (butylka), bottle

шесть (shest'), six — cognates

рубль (rubl'), ruble

съезд (s"jezd), descent, ramp — think of a sled going down a ramp

дочь (doch'), daughter — cognates

пять (pyat'), five — cognate with penta-, as in pentathlon, pentagram

опыт (opyt), experience — Opt for experience!

десять (desyat'), ten — cognate with decade and French dix

выход (vykhod), exit — the two words bear some similarities, with the x in the middle and the d/t at the end

музыка (muzyka), music

король (korol'), king — from German Karl, from Charlemagne

List 3

дым (dym), smoke — Smoke makes things dim

соль (sol'), salt

объяснить (ob"jyasnit'), to explain — It's obvious!

большой (bol'shoy), large, important — like the Bolshoi Ballet company

тридцать (tridtsat'), thirty — три + де́сять

целый (tselyy), intact, whole, entire — cognate with whole, I've got a whole jelly!

странный (strannyy), strange

холодный (kholodnyy), cold, cool — may be cognate

быть (byt'), to be

площадь (plóščad'), square, area, Красная площадь — Krásnaja plóščad' — Red Square, think of plaza

сечь (séč'), to whip, to cut — think of secateurs, also cognate with segment, To cut into segments

вещь (vesh'), thing — cognate with voice, The thing is spoken of, it's voiced

небольшой (nebol'shoy), small, not great

семь (sem'), seven — cognates

роль (rol'), role

вечный (véčnyj), eternal, perpetual — cognate with vanquish

печь (peč'), to bake, to scorch (sun) — Parch it in the sun

слабый (slábyj), feeble, flabby, infirm — think of a slob

данный (dannyy), given, present — The donation was given

жечь (žeč'), to burn, hot — cognate with day, Check the heat

Printed in Great Britain
by Amazon

36012675R00053